AMERICAN

For

MW01200883

BOOK ONE

EDITOR OF LOWER GRADE READERS
EDITH M. McLAUGHLIN

Former Critic Teacher, Parker Practice School,
Normal School, Chicago, Ill.

EDITOR OF UPPER GRADE READERS
T. ADRIAN CURTIS, A.B., LL.B.

District Superintendent, formerly Principal, Alexander Hamilton
Junior High School, New York

ASSOCIATE EDITORS

SISTER MARY AMBROSE, O.S.D., A.M.
(Supervisor)
St. Joseph's College and Academy,
Adrian, Michigan

SISTER MARY GERTRUDE, A.M.
Former Supervisor of Parochial High Schools,
Sisters of Charity, Convent Station
New Jersey

SISTER JAMES STANISLAUS
Former Supervisor of Parochial Schools,
Sisters of St. Joseph of Carondolet, St. Louis

ARTHUR H. QUINN, PH.D., LITT.D.
Professor of English, University of
Pennsylvania

TAN Books
Gastonia, North Carolina

Nihil Obstat:
        Arthur J. Scanlan, S.T.D.
        Censor Librorum

Imprimatur:
        ✠ Patrick Cardinal Hayes
        Archbishop of New York

American Cardinal Readers were originally published in 1950 and reprinted in 2013 by Neumann Press, an imprint of TAN Books.

Typesetting and minor revisions and corrections in *American Cardinal Readers: Book 1* © 2021 TAN Books

ISBN: 978-0911845-36-5
Kindle ISBN: 978-1-5051-0518-6
ePUB ISBN: 978-1-5051-0809-5

Published in the United States by
TAN Books
PO Box 269
Gastonia, NC 28053
www.TANBooks.com

Printed in the United States of America

CONTENTS

JEAN'S SURPRISE

It was morning. It was time
for Father to go to his work.

Mother and the children
were at the door with Father.
They were saying "Good-by" to him.

1

As Father started off, Jean said,
"When you come home to-night,
I shall have a surprise for you.
Mother and John are helping me
to get it ready for you, Father."

Father said, "That will be fine, Jean.
I shall be glad to see it to-night."

"O Father," said Jean, "it is not
a surprise for you to see.
It is something for you to hear."

"I can guess that," said Father.
"You are going to sing for me."

John said, "That is not it, Father."

Jean said, "You did not guess it
that time, Father."

2

Then Father laughed and said,
"I could guess it if I had time,
but I must go now, Jean.
Good-by, and God bless you all."

"Good-by, Father,"
said the children.
"God bless you, too," said Mother,
as Father walked away.

3

Jean worked hard that day
getting the surprise ready.

John helped her all he could.
Sometimes Mother had to help her.

When Father came home that night
the fine surprise was ready,
as Jean said it would be.

4

Mother had told Jean the best time
for the surprise was after dinner.

It was hard for her to wait
so long, but she did.

As soon as dinner was over,
Mother said, "Jean, it is time
for Father's surprise now."

"The book is in the next room.
I shall run and get it," said Jean.
Mother said, "Wait for us, Jean.
We are all going into that room."

As Father walked with Jean, he said,
"You are too little to read, Jean.
Why do you need a book?"

"My surprise is in a book, Father,"
said Jean with a kind smile.

Jean waited for Father, Mother
and John to take chairs.

Then she went over to a table
and took up the book she needed.

She said, "Father, this is the book
Grandmother and Grandfather
gave to John and me.
At first I could not read
the story in it, but I can now.
That is my surprise for you."

Then Jean began to read her story.
It was about the shepherds
who went to Bethlehem
the night Jesus was born.

Jean's surprise pleased Father.

He said, "Jean, I am so glad
you can read that beautiful story.
I know you have worked hard
to give me this surprise.
Thank you for it, Jean dear."

Jean said, "Mother and John
worked hard on the surprise, too.
They had to help me with the story
over and over again, Father."

Father smiled at Mother and John.
He looked so kind as he said,
"You have all made me happy.
Thank you for the beautiful story."

Mother said, "We are all glad
you liked Jean's surprise, Father."

WHAT JOHN WANTED TO KNOW

Father liked to read the paper
at night, after his dinner.
John liked to be Father's paper boy.

So when Jean's story was over,
John ran out of the room.
Before long, he came back
with the paper for Father.

As Father took the paper, he said,
"You are a fine paper boy, John.
You bring the paper to me,
just when I am ready to read."

John said,
"May I ask you something
before you begin to read, Father?"

"Yes, you may, John," said Father.

10

John asked, "Did the angel
tell anyone but the shepherds
where Jesus was born?"

"No, John. The angel went
only to the shepherds," said Father.

"Then the shepherds
must have been the only people
who went to Bethlehem," said John.

Father said,
"No, John, they were not.
Some other good men went there,
to find dear little Jesus.
God did not send an angel
to tell them where Jesus was.
He let them know in another way."

"O Father, please tell us about it,"
said John and Jean.

12

Father looked at his watch.

"It is near your bedtime, now.
I shall have to tell you the story
to-morrow night," he said.

"Thank you, Father," said Jean.
John said, "I shall be glad
when to-morrow night comes."

Then the children ran off
to get ready for bed.

The next night
Father told the children the story.
It is the next story in this book.

THE STORY FATHER TOLD

Long ago there lived some wise men. They were good men who loved God above all things.

These wise men knew many things
about the stars.
They knew the names of some stars.
They knew where to look in the sky
to find these stars.

The wise men wanted to know more
about the stars.
So they watched them
night after night
to find out all they could.

Many times when the wise men
were watching the stars,
they thought of a promise.
It was a beautiful promise.
It was a promise God had made.

God's promise was that a King
should be born.

This King was to rule
over all people.
He was to help the people
love and obey God
in all ways.

One night the wise men
were watching the stars.

It was near the time
God said the King should come.

All at once the wise men
saw something happen.
A beautiful new star
came into the sky.
The wise men had never seen
such a bright star.

The wise men looked and looked
at the beautiful new star.

Then they thought of
God's promise,
and their hearts were glad.
They were sure they knew now,
why this star had come.

They were sure it came to show
that the King God promised
was born.

They were sure, too, it was
near the place where He was born.

So the wise men got ready
to go in search
of the new-born King.

When the wise men were ready,
they rode away on camels.
They took beautiful gifts
with them.
The gifts were for the new King.

19

The wise men rode all that day.
When night came they looked
for the beautiful new star.
It was not in the sky.

The wise men rode many days
and many nights.
They looked for the new star,
night after night.
It was not in the sky.

After their long, long ride,
the wise men came to a town.

They asked the people in the town,
where the new King had been born.

The people could not tell them,
so the wise men rode away.

The wise men rode to a big city.
They said to the people there,
"Where is He Who is born King?
We have seen His star in the East
and are come to adore Him."

The people were surprised
by what the wise men asked.
They had not heard
that a new King was born.

These people knew of God's promise.
They thought of that promise now.
They talked to one another
about it.

They said, "This new King
may be the One,
God said would come."

23

Herod lived in this big city.
He was the king of the country.
He was very wicked.

Herod had heard
what the wise men were asking.
He had heard what the people
were saying to one another.

Herod thought this new King
must be the One, God promised.
He knew the King, God promised,
was to rule over all people.

It made Herod very, very angry
when he thought about this.
He said to himself, "No other king
shall take my place. I will find
this new-born King and kill Him."

Herod had to know first
where God said
the new King should be born.

There were some men in the city
who could tell Herod this.
Herod sent for these men.

The men came.
They told Herod, the new King
was to be born in Bethlehem.
Then they went away.

Then Herod sent for the wise men.
He let no one know he did this.
He did not want anyone to know
he was trying to find the new King.
He was afraid
the people would find out
he was going to kill the King.

When the wise men came,
he talked with them
about the star they had seen.
He asked them
when they had seen it.
He talked with them, too,
about the King they came to find.

No one could have told
Herod wanted to kill the new King.

27

Herod told the wise men,
they would find the new King
in Bethlehem.

Then he said to them,
"Go and look well for the Child.
When you have found Him, come back
and tell me where He is.
Then I, too, shall go
and adore Him."

It was night when the wise men
rode away from Herod's palace.

Soon they were out of the city.
Just then the beautiful new star
came into the sky again.
How happy the wise men were
to see it once more!

29

The star went before the wise men,
until it came and stood over
where the Child was.

The wise men may have thought
they should find the new-born King
in a beautiful palace.

The star was not over a palace.
It was over a poor home.
The wise men went into
this poor home.

"They found the Child
with Mary, His Mother.
And, falling down, they adored Him."

The wise men gave the little King
the gifts they had for Him.
Then they went away.

The wise men did not go back
to Herod.

One night when they were sleeping,
God let them know
they were not to go back to him.

So they went back another way
into their country.

The wise men had never been
so happy as they were now.
They had found the new-born King
and they had adored Him.

The King was Jesus, God's Son.

A WINTER DAY

One morning Jean said to John,
"I wish it would snow to-day.
Then you and I could take out
our new sled and play with it."

"I wish it would snow, too.
I want to give you a fine ride
on the new sled first, Jean.
Then I want to see if I can
go down hill fast on it," said John.

Mother was in the room and heard
what the children said.
She walked to the window
and looked out.
It was snowing.

35

Mother said, "O children, come here!
See what is falling from the sky."

Jean and John ran to the window
as fast as they could.

Jean said, "Snowflakes! Snowflakes!
How fast they are coming down!
Now we can take out our sled, John."

John said, "It will be fun
to have these big round snowflakes
fall on us as we play."

Mother asked, "Do the snowflakes look round to you, John?"

John said, "Yes, Mother, they do."

Jean said,
"They look round to me, too.
They are round, are they not?"

Mother said, "I have a glass that will help you to find out.
It is a glass to look through.
Things seem large when you look at them through this glass.
Let us all go outdoors and look at the snowflakes through it."

Soon Jean and John were ready.
Mother and Baby were ready, too.
Then they all went outdoors.

Down, down, down, came the snow.
A snowflake fell on John's arm.
Mother put the glass over it.
Jean and John looked through
the glass.

"This snowflake is not round.
It looks like a star," said Jean.

"It looks like a star to me, too.
It has six points," said John.

Jean and John looked at many
snowflakes through the glass.
All the snowflakes were like stars.
They were stars with six points.

John said, "Thank you, Mother,
for helping Jean and me find out
what a snowflake is like."

39

Then Mother, Baby, Jean and John
went into the house.

Soon John and Jean came out again.
They had their fine new sled.

"If you want a good ride,
get on the sled, Jean," said John.

Jean sat down on the sled.
"Now run fast, John," said Jean.
John did run fast. He gave Jean
a fine ride.

"Let us go over to the hill now.
I shall watch you, John,
as you ride down fast," said Jean.

So John and Jean went to the hill.
What fun it was for John
to ride down-hill very fast!

Soon Jean said, "Let me do that, too. I am not afraid to ride down-hill."

So down the hill the children rode. Then they had to get off the sled and climb to the top of the hill. They did this again and again.

When playtime was over, Jean said, "When the snow stars come, children have fun."

41

THE SNOWMAN

The next morning Jean and John went out to play in the snow again.

"Let us make a snowman," said John.
"If Paul and Anne would help us, we could make a big one," said Jean.
"You run and ask Anne to help us. I shall ask Paul," said John.

So off ran Jean and John.

John and Paul came back first.
Soon the girls came running back.

"Now we can go to work," said John.
"First we must make two snowballs.
We must have a big snowball
for the head and a very big one
for the body."

Anne said, "I want to make
the snowball for the head, John."

"I want to help Anne," said Jean.

John said, "That is fine, girls.
You make the snowball for the head.
Paul and I shall make the one
for the body."

The children went to work at once.

Jean and Anne had to roll and roll the snow to make the big snowball for the snowman's head.

John and Paul had to roll and roll and roll and roll the snow to make the very big snowball for the body.

At last the snowballs were ready.

The boys put the snowman's head
on his body.

"That does not look like
a snowman. It looks like two big
snowballs, one on top of the other,"
said Jean.

The children laughed and Paul said,
"We have not finished our work.
We have many things to do, Jean,
before this will look like a man."

"We have so many things to do, we must not stop to talk," said John.

"First, the snowman must have eyes. Who will find something to make his eyes?"

"Let us do that," said the girls. "I shall make his mouth," said Paul. "I shall make his nose," said John. Soon they all were at work.

All at once Paul saw his dog.

"Here comes my dog. He is looking for me," said Paul.

"Run and hide from him," said John. "Let us see if he can find you."

"Hide behind the snowman," said Anne.

"Hide behind the snowman," said Jean.

So Paul ran behind the snowman.

The dog ran up to the children.
He went from one to the other.
He looked this way and that way.

He barked, "Bow-wow! Bow-wow!"
That was his way of asking them,
"Will you tell me where Paul is?"

"Lad, go and find Paul," said John.
"You will find him if you look."

Lad just stood and barked.

48

Then Paul called,
"Come, Lad, come!"
Lad looked over at the snowman.
"Bow-wow! Bow-wow!" he barked and
over to the snowman he ran.

He ran right into the snowman.
Down went the snowman's big head.
The snow went all over Paul.
How Paul and the children laughed!

Lad was so glad to find Paul,
that he ran around and around him.
When he stopped running,
he put his nose in Paul's hand.
That made the children laugh.

"See what he does next," said Paul.
Just then Lad took Paul's hand
in his mouth.

"Lad will hurt you," said Jean.
"He will not hurt me," said Paul.
"He is just trying to take me home.
Mother must have sent him for me.
I must go now, but I will help
to make another snowman some day."

"I must go, too. Mother said to play
just a little while," said Anne.
So all the children said "Good-by."
Playtime was over for that day.

HOW THE SNOW HELPS

That night when Father came home,
Jean and John told him all about
the snowman they had made.

They told him about Lad, too.
Father laughed when he heard
what Lad did to the snowman.

Father said to Jean and John,
"You can make another snowman.
Winter will last for many days,
so there will be snow to play in
for a long time."

"I am glad winter is going to last
for a long time," said Jean.
"I do like to play in the snow."

"I guess we have snow just so
children can play in it," said John.

Father said, "No, John, the snow
does not come so that children
may have fun playing in it.
A very long time ago,
when I was a little boy,
Grandmother told me why it comes."

54

"Grandmother knows
so many things.
Please tell us what she told you
about the snow, Father," said John.

So Father said to the children:
    "God sends the snow
    To cover trees
    And all the sleeping flowers,
    To keep the cold
    From little seeds
    That some day will be flowers."

"I know now why the snow comes.
It has work to do," said John.

"That is right, John," said Father.
"God has work for us to do, and
everything He sends has work to do."

ANNE'S BIRTHDAY PARTY

One day when the children ran in from outdoors, Jean said to Mother, "I am so sorry for Anne, Mother. Her birthday will be here soon. She was going to have a party, but her grandmother is sick, so she can not have it."

John said, "Anne has never had a party on her birthday, Mother. That is why Jean and I are sorry she can not have one this time. Anne is not so sorry about the birthday party as she is about her grandmother."

Mother said, "I shall go to see
Anne's sick grandmother now.
While I am over at Anne's house,
I shall ask her mother if we may
have a party for Anne here."

"How kind you are, Mother,"
said the children as they put
their arms around her.

Mother came back. The children were waiting at the door for her.

"What did Anne's mother say? Please tell us, Mother," said John.

"Yes, please tell us," said Jean.

"Anne's mother told me
that the dear grandmother is going
to get well," said Mother.
She will not be well in time
for Anne to have a party at home.
The party will be at our house.
I asked Anne's mother not to say
a thing to Anne about it."

"Good for you, Mother! We can have a surprise party now," said John.
"Anne will like that," said Jean.

Mother said,
"We must get ready
for our party. First we must ask
the children to come. How many
do you want to have?"

Jean said, "Mother, Anne will be
seven years old, so let us have
seven children at the party."

John said, "We shall have to ask
four children. Four with Anne,
Jean and me will make seven.
We shall have Anne, Mary, Margaret,
Paul and Joseph at the party."

Jean laughed and said, "We have
no other friends to ask, Mother."

"I am glad all your little friends
can be asked to come," said Mother.

The next day Jean and John took
party cards to all their friends
but Anne.

This is what it said on the card:

We are going to have a party,
To surprise our little friend Anne
Two, on Saturday, is the time,
So be with us then if you can.

Jean and John.

At last the party day came.
Mary, Joseph, Margaret and Paul
went to the party early.

John said to his little friends,
"We are glad you came early.
Anne has not come yet."

Jean said, "Anne thinks she is
coming over just to show me
her new birthday book."
The children laughed to think
what a surprise Anne would have.

"Here comes Anne now," said Paul.
Jean said, "Run and hide some place.
I have to go and let Anne in.
When Anne comes into the room,
call out, 'Surprise on Anne!' "

The children ran here and there
to find good places to hide.
Then Jean went to the door.

Jean and Anne came into the room.
The children ran from their places
calling, "Surprise! Surprise on Anne!"
Anne was surprised.

Mother came in and said,
"I heard you calling 'Surprise!'
That told me it was time to come
and help you sing 'Happy Birthday.'
Let us make a ring now."

So the children made a big ring
around Anne, and Mother helped them
sing this:

"You are seven years old to-day,
Seven years old, seven years old,
You are seven years old to-day,
So we sing 'Happy Birthday' to you."

65

Then the children played games.
Mother told them about a new game.
She said, "Come and stand before me.
When I say 'stoop,' you must stand.
When I say 'stand,' you must stoop.
If I catch you, you have to be 'it'. "

The children got ready to play.
Mother said, "I say – – – stoop!"
Down went Paul at once.
"Paul let me catch him," said Mother.

Paul had to be "it" then.
He said, "I say – – – stand!"
Down they all went but Anne,
so she had to be "it."

The children had a good time
playing the game over and over.

After the games, Mother took
the children into another room.
There was a table in this room
with seven chairs around it.

Mother said, "Now find your places.
There is a card at each place.
Each card has a name on it.
The card that has your name
is at your place."

Mother put the birthday cake
on the table. The seven candles
on the cake gave a bright light.

Mother let the children
blow out the candles.
Then she cut the cake.

She gave each child some cake
and some ice cream, too.

69

After that, Jean gave each child
a little basket with candy in it.

John gave Anne a very big basket.
There was a walking doll in it.

First Anne thanked Jean, John
and their mother for the doll.
Then she showed the children
how it walked.

Anne's birthday party was over.
The children got ready to go home.
Each child went to Mother and said,
"I thank you for the happy time
I had at the party to-day."

Then the children said "Good-by"
to one another and went home.

WHAT FATHER KELLY TOLD

One Saturday morning John said, "The boys are going to play ball this morning, Mother. Please may I go and play with them?"

"John, there is so much work to do, I need your help this morning. I need Jean's help, too," said Mother.

Jean said, "I am ready to help. I wanted to play with the girls this morning, but I can do that after I have helped you, Mother."

John did not say a word, but he looked very, very cross.

"Why are you so cross, John?"
asked Mother.

John said, "I always have to help.
Some boys never have to help.
They have all their time for play.
I should like to play all day, too."

"O John," said Jean, "Father Kelly
would not like to hear you
say that to Mother. You know
what he told us at Mass on Sunday."

"What did Father Kelly say, Jean?
I should like to hear what he told
the children," said Mother.

Jean said to her mother,
"Father Kelly told us what to do
to honor our fathers and mothers.
He told us why we should honor them.
This is what he said, Mother:

"My dear children, always love
your fathers and your mothers.
Do all you can to make them happy.

"Be ready to do as your fathers
and your mothers wish you to do.
They love you, so they ask you
to do only what is best for you.

"You honor your fathers and mothers
by doing as they wish you to do.
You honor them when you do
what will make them happy.

"You please God when you honor
your fathers and your mothers.
God wishes you to honor them.
Long, long ago He said,
'Honor thy father and thy mother.' "

When Jean had told
all that Father Kelly said,
John ran over to his mother
and put his arms around her.

He said, "O Mother, I am so sorry
I was cross about having to help.
I know I have not pleased God.
I know I have not made you happy.
I am very, very sorry.

"After this, I will always try to do
as you wish me to do, Mother.
Then God will know I love Him
and want to please Him.

"I want to help you, now, Mother.
Please forgive me for being cross
at first."

Mother said, "God forgives us
when we tell Him we are sorry
for not doing as He wishes us to do.

"He is always ready to help us
do better, when we ask Him
to help us.

"He knows you are sorry you did not
please Him this morning, John.
He will forgive you and help you
to be a better boy, next time.

"I shall forgive you, too, John.
We should forgive one another
as God forgives us.

"I am glad you want to help now.
Come! I shall show you and Jean
what to do to help me."

Soon John and Jean were at work.
They worked so well it did not
take them very long to finish
what they had to do.

Mother said, "You have been
good helpers, Jean and John.
You may go and play, now."

The children ran off to play.
Jean played house with the girls.
John played ball with the boys.
His team won the game.

JOSEPH'S SURPRISE

Once Joseph went to John's house and called, "O John! O John!"

"Joseph is calling you," John. "See what he wants," said Mother.

So John ran to the door to see what his little friend wanted.

As soon as John had the door open
Joseph said, "John, ask your mother
if you and Jean may come over
to my house. I have something new
I want you to see."

John went and asked his mother.
Mother said, "Jean and you may go."

So the children went with Joseph.

"Anne, Mary, Margaret and Paul must see what I have," said Joseph. "Let us stop at their houses and call for them."

So Jean, John and Joseph stopped first at one house, then at another, and at another and at another.

At last the seven little friends were on their way to Joseph's house.

As the children walked along
Paul said, "Joseph, tell us something
about this thing you have.
We shall try to guess what it is."

Joseph said, "It is something with
two ears, two eyes, a nose, a mouth
and four legs."

"It is a dog," said Paul and John.
"Yes, it must be a dog," said Anne.
"It may be a horse," said Jean.
"It may be a cat," said Margaret.

"Each of those animals has a nose,
a mouth, two eyes, two ears and
four legs, but not one of them
is what I have," said Joseph.
"Just wait! You will know soon."

85

Soon they were at Joseph's house.
Joseph said, "Come back to the yard.
That is where my big surprise is."

The children ran back to the yard.
There they saw a large cage and
in the cage were two white rabbits.

86

"Rabbits!" said the children. "May we take them in our arms?"

"Yes, you may, if you know how to pick them up," said Joseph.

"I do," said Paul, and he was going to pick up a rabbit by its ears. Joseph stopped him and said, "That is not the way to pick up a rabbit. Picking it up by the ears hurts it. My father told me so."

Paul asked, "Do you know the way we should pick them up, Joseph?" Joseph said, "My father showed me the right way, so I will show you."

The children watched to see how Joseph picked up the rabbit.

"This is the way," said Joseph, and he picked up one rabbit by the back of its neck.

"O," said Anne, "that is the way a mother cat picks up her kittens." Jean said, "A mother dog picks up the little dogs that way, too." "That is right, girls," said Joseph.

After the children had played with Joseph's rabbits for a while, it was time for them to go home.

"Thank you, Joseph, for showing us your white rabbits," they said. "When we come to see them again we will pick them up the right way – – – – by the back of the neck."

THE BLUE DISH

One day when Mother went away, Margaret, Mary and Anne came over with their dolls to play with Jean.

They were going to have a party. Jean had some cake for the party. Mary and Anne had some apples. Margaret had candy.

The girls helped Jean bring out her table, chairs and dishes. They put the table and chairs under the big tree. Then they put the dishes on the table.

"We have a dish for the cake and one for the apples," said Mary. "We must have another little one for the candy."

Jean said, "I have no more dishes.
Mother has a little blue dish.
I shall get that for the candy."

Anne said, "Jean, has your mother
ever let you play with her dish?"

"No, she has not," said Jean.

"Then you must not take it now
when your mother is away," said Anne.

"Anne is right, Jean," said Mary.

Margaret said, "We do not need
another dish. We can put the candy
with the apples, Jean."

"I do not want to do that.
I want the blue dish on our table.
I am going to get it," said Jean.

So she did.

When everything was ready
Jean said, "Now let us sit down."

The girls took their dolls
and sat down at the table.
They ate the apples and cake first.
Then they ate the candy.

Just before it was time to go home, Mary said, "Jean, we shall help you put the things away now."

"We shall help with everything but the blue dish," said Anne. "Jean should take care of that."

"I shall take care of it," said Jean. "You bring in the table and the chairs. I shall take the dish."

Jean was the first one to reach the house. As she looked around to see where the other girls were, she fell down. The dish fell too. "I broke the dish! I broke it!" said Jean, and she began to cry.

Her little friends ran to her and
told her how sorry they were.
Then they put everything away
and went home.
Jean went into the house.

Before long, Mother came home. John was there playing with Baby. Kate was there watching them. Kate was the big girl who came to help do the work some days.

When Mother did not see Jean, she said to Kate, "Where is Jean?"

"Jean is in her room," said Kate. "She went there after her playtime with the girls."

"She must be tired," said Mother. "We shall let her rest."

Jean heard everything Mother said. "I do not want Mother to think I am tired, for that is not true. I want to tell her about the dish but I can not do it now," she said.

Just then Jean heard Mother say,
"Kate, where is the blue dish?
I have some candy to put in it."

Kate did not know where it was.
She began to look for it.

All this time something seemed
to say to Jean, "Tell where it is!
Tell your mother now—right now!"

"I will tell now!" said Jean.
So she called her mother.

Mother went into Jean's room.
Jean said, "Mother, I took the dish
to play with it. When I was coming
into the house with it, I fell.
The blue dish fell, too, and broke.
I am so sorry I did it, Mother.
I am going to save my money
and buy you another one."

Then Mother said to Jean,
"I am sorry you took something
to play with that was not yours.
I am sorry you broke the dish.
I am glad you want to save
your money to buy a new one.
You have made me happy, Jean,
by telling me the true story."

Jean said, "Something seemed
to make me tell the true story.
I think it was my guardian angel."

"It was your angel," said Mother.

Mother and Jean were happy now.
Jean began that day to save
her money for the new dish.

WHEN FLAGS WERE FLYING

One morning Jean and John rose very early to help Father put out their big flag.

All the people who had flags put them out that day.

A great man was coming to the town and the people wished to have their flags flying when he came.

After Jean and John helped Father, they took a walk down the street. They wanted to see how many flags were flying and how they looked.

The children had not walked far when Joseph came up behind them. He wanted to see all the flags along the street, too, so he walked with Jean and John.

As they went along, Jean said, "A flag is flying from every house on this street."
John said, "We have not passed all the houses, Jean. We must walk to the end of the street to see if there is a flag at each house."

Before long, Jean, John and Joseph
came to the end of the street.
"Look at that last house," said John.
Jean and Joseph looked.
No flag was flying at that house.

The three children walked over
to the house and began to talk.

"The people in this last house
may not have a flag," said Jean.

John said, "They may not know
a great man is coming here to-day.
That may be why no flag is out."

"The people may not be at home
to put out a flag," said Joseph.

Just then the door was opened.
A very kind-looking old woman
came out of the house.

She walked over to the children.
"Good morning, children," she said.
"Good morning," said Jean.
"Good morning," said the boys,
as they took off their hats.

Then the kind old woman said,
"I heard you talking, so I came
to tell you why there is not
a flag flying at this house.

"I have a great, great big flag.
I can not put it out myself.
There is no one at home to-day
to help me put it out.
I am very sorry about it."

Joseph said, "I have a big brother
who could put out your big flag.
Shall I run home for him?"

"It would make me happy to have
my flag flying," said the woman.

Joseph ran home for his brother.
Jean and John ran with him.

Soon the three children came back
with Joseph's big brother.
The woman was waiting for them.

Joseph said, "This is my brother."
The brother said, "My name is James.
I have come to put out your flag."

The woman said, "You are very kind
to do this for me, James."
Then she took him into the house
to bring out her big flag.

When James came out with the flag,
he said, "You can help me, children.
See that I do not let the flag
touch the ground."

The children watched, but the flag
did not touch the ground once.

Soon James had the flag flying.

107

As they all looked up and
saw the flag flying, they said,
"This is the flag of our country,
The beautiful Red, White and Blue
Beautiful flag of our country,
To you we will always be true."

Then James said to the woman,
"I will come back before sundown
to take in your flag."

The woman said, "I am glad
you thought of that, James.
Our flag must not be out
after the sun goes down."

The new friends said "Good-by"
to one another. Then James and
the children started for home.

GOOD NEWS

Mother once said to Jean and John,
"I have some good news for you.
Grandmother and Grandfather
are coming for a visit."

"O good!" said Jean and John.
They were so happy they began
to jump up and down.

"I shall tell you more good news
if you will listen," said Mother.

Jean and John stopped jumping.
Then Mother said, "A boy is coming
with Grandmother and Grandfather.
His name is Frank and he is
about as big as you are, John.
They will all be here soon."

"Jean, you and I shall have to work
to get ready for Frank," said John.
"We must look over our toys.
We must think of things to do
to help Frank have a good time."

Jean said, "I am ready to help you."
So Jean and John began
to get ready for Frank's visit.

ONE HAPPY MORNING

That night Mother said to Father and the children, "We must all get up early in the morning. Grandmother, Grandfather and Frank are coming for their visit. They will be here early."

John said, "Father, are you going to the train to meet them?"

"Yes, I am, John," said Father. "May I go with you?" asked John. "May I go too, Father?" asked Jean.

"You may go if you are ready on time, children," said Father. "I must meet the train on time."

The next morning Jean and John were ready to go to the train before Father was.

"Good morning, little early birds," said Father when he saw them. "You have a joke on me now." Then they all laughed and laughed.

As soon as Father was ready, Jean and John jumped into the car with him and went to the train.

The car went on and on and on.
At last, Father stopped it and said,
"Grandmother's train comes in here.
You must wait in the car, children,
while I go out to the train."

So Jean and John waited in the car
while Father went to meet Frank,
Grandmother and Grandfather.

Jean and John watched the people as they came from the train.

Before long, they saw Father coming to the car with Grandmother, Grandfather and Frank.

John waved his hand to them. Jean waved her hand to them, too.

Grandmother and Grandfather saw the children and waved back.

Soon they were all in the car
and on the way home.

Then Jean and John began to talk
to their new little friend, Frank.
They told him
what they were going to do
to help him have a happy visit.

Before they knew it, they were home.
Mother and Baby came out to meet
Grandmother, Grandfather
and Frank.   They were glad
to see one another.

Grandfather said, "How that baby
is growing!   Do let me take her!"

Mother gave Grandfather the baby.
Then they all went into the house
to talk and rest for a while.

117

GRANDFATHER'S JOKE

After Jean and John showed Frank
all their toys, Grandfather said,
"Frank and I have something
to show you now, that you have
never seen before."

"I will get it," said Frank, and
off he ran.

Soon Frank came back and put
a nest into Grandfather's hands.
It was an old nest that the birds
had left when the days grew cold.

When John saw it, he said,
"O Grandfather! We have seen
a nest before. We have seen
many, many nests."

"I want you and Jean to look at this nest," said Grandfather. "I think it is not just like those you have seen in town here."

The children looked at the nest. "Grandfather, I can see some wool in this nest," said John.

"I see some wool, too," said Jean. "Where did the birds get it?"

Grandfather laughed and said, "They got it from the bushes, Jean."

John said, "How could the birds get wool from a bush, Grandfather? Wool comes from the sheep."

"Frank will tell you about that," said Grandfather. So Frank did.

"A brook runs through the farm
where I live," said Frank.
"Bushes grow all along its banks.
The farm animals drink good water
from it every day.

"One day the cows and the horses went to the brook for a drink. They walked right over the bushes to reach the water.

"The sheep were in a field near by. They saw the cows and horses getting a drink at the brook.

" 'Baa! Baa!' went an old sheep. That was his way of saying, 'We must have some water, too. Come over to the brook with me.'

"So the other sheep left the field and walked behind the old sheep, over to the little brook.

"The sheep could not walk over
the tall bushes around the brook.
They had to walk through them.

"The wool of one sheep caught
on a branch of a big bush.
The wool of another sheep caught
on the branch of another bush.
Soon the bushes looked as if
little wool flowers were growing
on them.

"Two birds were in a tree near by.
They were at work making a nest.
They looked down and saw the wool
that had caught on the bushes.
They came flying down for it.
They took it back to the tree
and put it in the new nest.

"This nest was a very good home
for their little baby birds.
The wool made it soft and warm."

When Frank had finished his story
he gave the nest to John.
"Show this to the girls and boys
you know, John, and tell them
about the wool in it," he said.
John thanked Frank for the nest.

Then Grandfather said to Jean,
"Was I right when I told you
the wool came from the bushes?"

Jean said, "Yes, you were right.
I see your joke now, Grandfather.
The birds did get the wool
from the bushes, but the bushes
got it from the sheep."

Then they all had a good laugh
over Grandfather's joke.

FEEDING JOSEPH'S RABBITS

Jean and John took Frank to see
Joseph's two white rabbits.
When the children came near them,
one rabbit sat up on his hind legs.

Jean said, "Look at him, Frank!
Did you ever before see a rabbit
sit up on his hind legs?"

Frank said, "Yes, I did, Jean.
I have seen many rabbits
sit up on their hind legs.
Other animals sit up that way, too.

"I have a little squirrel
down in the country. He lives
in an old tree right by my house.
When he wants something to eat
he runs to me and sits up
on his hind legs."

Joseph said, "Your squirrel is like my rabbit, Frank. He sits up when he wants something to eat."

"Then your rabbit must want something to eat now," said Frank. "Let us see what we can find."

The children looked all around and soon found some white clover.

As they came back with the clover, the other rabbit sat up.
"This rabbit likes clover, too.
Please give him some," said John.

The children gave some clover to each rabbit. It was fun to watch the rabbits bite off the clover with their sharp teeth.

A GOOD RACE

When the children were going home
from Joseph's house, they saw Paul
down the street.   Lad was with him.

All at once Paul and Lad
saw the children and ran
as fast as they could to meet them.

Lad did not know Frank.
He barked and barked at him.

Paul said, "Stop that, Lad. Do not
bark at Frank.   He is John's friend.
Go and shake hands with him."

Frank stooped over and said,
"Shake hands, Lad! Shake hands!"
Lad put his paw into Frank's hand.
"Good dog! Good dog!" said Frank.

133

"He is a fine dog," said Jean. "He plays with us all the time and never hurts us."

"He can run fast, too," said John. "He can run as fast as I can."

"I think he can run faster than we can, John," said Paul. "Let us have a race and see. Let us race to my house."

Jean said, "I shall not race, but I shall tell you when to go."

When the boys and Lad were ready, Jean said, "One-two-three! Go!"

Off went the boys. Off went Lad. Lad was soon ahead of the boys, but he kept running on and on.

Frank called him back and said,
"You won, Lad! You won the race."

"Bow-wow! Bow-wow!" barked Lad,
as if to say, "I am glad I did."

JEAN'S SHEEP

The next day Jean said to Frank,
"Please come and see our sheep.
They are not like the sheep
you have in the country.
They never eat and they never say
'Baa! Baa! Baa!'"

"I never heard of sheep like those.
I want to see them," said Frank.

Jean said, "We keep our sheep
on a big blue hill, Frank.
Sometimes they stand very still
on this big blue hill, but
when the wind blows, they walk
and walk and walk.
See, there they are now!"

Jean pointed to the blue sky.
Frank looked at the sky and saw
some soft white clouds there.
He looked and looked at the clouds.
At last he said, "Those clouds
do look like sheep, Jean."

"They are still now," said Jean,
"but they will walk just as soon
as the wind blows. Watch them!"

Frank watched the cloud sheep
while Jean said this:

"White sheep, white sheep
On a blue hill.
When the wind stops
You all stand still.

You walk far away
When the winds blow;
White sheep, white sheep,
Where do you go?"

"I like your cloud sheep, Jean.
I wish I could put my hands
on them," said Frank.

"I wish I could do that, too,
but we cannot climb up to the hill,"
said Jean, laughing.

138

TWO CAREFUL BOYS

One morning John's mother
wanted something from the store.

"Let me go to the store for you.
I will be very careful, Mother.
I will look first one way and
then the other before I cross
the street," said John.

"Please let me go, too," said Frank.
So Mother let the boys go.

The boys walked to the corner
and came to the car tracks.
John stopped, so Frank stopped.
The boys looked up the street,
but saw nothing coming.
When they looked down the street,
they saw a street car coming.

While the boys waited for it
to pass, Frank said to John,
"I have never had a long ride
on a street car."

"You will have one, some day.
Come, we may cross now," said John.

So the boys crossed the street
and went on to the store to get
what John's mother wanted.

On the way back from the store,
they stopped at the corner again.
A car was coming along one track.
Another car was coming along
the other track.
The boys waited for them to pass.

A man crossed the street when
John and Frank did.
He looked at them and said,
"You are two careful boys.
I saw you wait at the corner
for the street cars to pass.
I like boys that do things
the way they should."

"Thank you," said Frank and John.
Then they ran home to John's mother.

A STREET CAR RIDE

When John told his mother
that Frank never had a long ride
on a street car, she said,
"Let us go for one to-day, then.
Tell Frank and Jean we shall go
as soon as we can get ready.
Ask Grandmother and Grandfather
if they would like to go."

John asked Grandmother and Grandfather first.

Grandmother said she would not go because she did not like to ride.

Grandfather said he would go because he could help Mother and the children on and off the cars.

Jean and Frank were so happy when they heard the good news, they began to clap their hands.

Before long, Mother, Grandfather, and the children were on the car.

Jean and John found a place for Frank next to the window. "We want you to see everything as you ride along," said Jean. "Thank you, Jean," said Frank.

On and on went the street car. It passed many, many houses. It passed many stores, too.

Frank said, "A town has houses, stores and street cars, but it has no big green fields. It has not so many trees, birds, and flowers as the country has."

146

147

Just then the car stopped.
"This is as far as the car goes.
We get off here," said Mother.

When Grandfather helped them
off the car, the children saw
they were right at the big park.

"O Mother!" said Jean and John,
"are we going to see the animals?"

"Yes," said Mother. "I think
that will be fun for Frank."

Jean said, "It will be fun for us
to see the animals, too, Mother."

So, laughing and talking, they went
through the big park to the place
where the animals were kept.

148

AT THE PARK

There were two big elephants
in the park, and the children
went to see them first.

As the children came near,
one elephant put out his trunk.
Then the other elephant put out
his trunk.

"They want something to eat, but
we have nothing for them," said John.

Mother said to John,
"Read that sign over there.
Then you will know why we did not
bring something for the animals."

John looked at the sign. It said,
"Please do not feed the animals."

A big boy, standing near,
heard Mother tell John to look
at the sign, so he looked at it, too.

Then he turned to John's mother
and showed her two big apples.
"I was going to give the apples
to the elephants, but now
I will not," he said.

All at once, one of the elephants
put out his long trunk and
took an apple from the boy's hand.
How the children laughed!

"Well, big elephant," said the boy,
"I did not feed you, that time.
You just helped yourself."

PLEASE
DO NOT FEED
THE ANIMALS

Mother took the children
to the lions' cage next.
A mother lion and two baby lions
were in the cage.

One baby lion sat in the corner
of the cage all the time, but
the other one did something
that made the children laugh.

The mother lion was very still
when the children came to the cage.
After a while, she began to move
her tail from side to side.

The baby lion saw the tail move
and jumped after it.
He jumped, first to one side,
then to the other side, but
he could not catch the tail.

Then all at once he gave
a big jump and over he rolled.
He looked like a big soft ball
as he rolled over and over.

The children laughed and laughed.
Then this baby lion went and sat
in the corner of the cage, too.

In a cage not far from the lions were two big tigers.
As the children came to the cage, they saw a man give some meat to the tigers.

"Mother, tell that man he must not feed the animals," said Jean.

Mother laughed and said, "That man has a right to feed the animals, Jean. He is called the keeper and it is his work to feed all the animals here."

Frank asked, "Does the keeper know just what to feed each animal?"
"Yes, he does, Frank," said Mother. "He knows when to feed each one, too."

"People do not always know
what is best for the animals.
That is why the sign says,
'Please do not feed the animals.'"

Grandfather looked at his watch. "Come, it is getting late, and we have not seen the bears and the camels," he said.

The children left the tigers' cage and went to see the two big camels and the baby camel.

The children liked the baby camel best of all. When his mother walked around, he walked with her. When she stood still, he stood, too.

Once the mother and baby camel stood so near the children that the baby camel looked down at them. Just then the keeper came along with some hay.

The mother went to get some hay,
but the baby did not see her go.

All at once he turned his head.
He saw his mother walking away,
so he ran to catch up with her.

The children laughed and laughed
to see him run on his long legs.

Jean, John and Frank went to see
the bears last of all.
When the children came near them,
the bears stood on their hind legs.

"We know what you want, big bears.
You want us to feed you, but
the keeper must do that," said John.

Just then the keeper came along
with some meat for the bears.
When Frank saw the meat, he said
to the keeper, "Do you give meat
to the bears always?"

"No, I do not," said the keeper.
"Sometimes I give them bread
and sometimes I give them fish.
Bears like bread, fish and meat."

160

Then the keeper threw the meat
to the bears, so that the children
could see them catch it.

When all the bears had been fed,
the children were ready to go home.
They were tired but happy.

THE BIG STORE

On the last day of Frank's visit, Mother took him and the children to see the big stores downtown.

As they went into one store Mother said, "We are going up to the floor where the toys are, so we shall take the elevator."

John and Jean had been in an elevator many times before. This was Frank's first ride in one, and he liked it.

The elevator went up so fast, he was surprised when it stopped to let them off at the floor where they were to see the toys.

Mother and the three children walked around looking at things.

They saw toy animals of all kinds that looked just like real animals.

They saw things that all boys like— balls, bats and catching gloves.

They saw things that girls like— dolls, dishes, tables and chairs.

Once they stopped to watch a toy train that was running on a track, going through hills and doing all the things that a real train does.

"I wish I had a train and a track just like that," said John.
"So do I," said Frank.

164

When Jean and the boys had seen
all the toys, Mother took them
to the big playroom in the store.

Many children were in the room.
Some were playing on a slide.
Some were going up and down
on a see-saw and others were
on rocking-horses.

Mother said, "You may play here
while I go and buy some things
Grandmother wants."

Jean and the boys went into
the big playroom. By the time
Mother came back, each one
had been on a slide, a see-saw
and a rocking-horse.

As Frank, Jean and John were going out of the store with Mother, Frank saw some cards on a table near the door.

He pointed to them and said, "There are pictures on those cards. I should like to see them." So Mother, Jean and John stopped to look at the cards with him.

There were cards with pictures of the downtown streets and stores. There were cards with pictures of the animals in the big park. There were cards with pictures of many places in the city.

"I am going to buy some cards
for my mother and my father.
They could not come to the city,
so they will like to see pictures
that tell about it," said Frank.

When Mother, Jean and John
had helped Frank pick out
the best pictures, it was time
to go home.

THE END OF THE VISIT

When the time came for Frank, Grandmother and Grandfather to go to the train, Frank said to Father, "I wish Jean and John were going to the train with us."

"I think there is room in the car, not only for Jean and John, but for Mother and Baby," said Father.

When the children heard Father say this, they were so very happy they began to jump up and down and to clap their hands.

Then they went with Mother to get ready for the ride.

Before long, they were all
on the way to the train.

As the car was going along,
Frank thanked Mother, Father,
Grandmother and Grandfather for
his happy visit to the city.

He asked Jean and John to come
to the country to visit him.
"I want you to have as good a time
in the country as I have had
in the city," he said.

Soon Father stopped the car.
"Come, Grandmother, Grandfather
and Frank. This is the place
you get your train," he said.

When they had all said "Good-by,"
Father helped Grandmother, Frank
and Grandfather to the train.
Then he came back and took Mother,
Baby, Jean and John home.

A PRAYER

While John was getting ready
for bed that night, he thought
of the happy times Jean and he had
when Frank was visiting them.

He thought of all the places
Mother had taken them to.
He thought of the good long rides
they had taken with Father.
He thought of their good home.
He thought of the happy playtimes
they had had with their little friends.

He said, "Jean and I should say
our 'Thank You' prayer to-night.
Jean may not have thought of it."

He went to the door of Jean's room and told her what he had been thinking about.

Then he said to her, "After you say your night prayers, Jean, please say the 'Thank You' prayer. I am going to say it, too."

"I will do that, John," said Jean.

Jean and John said this prayer:

For Father and Mother
So loving and kind,
Dear Heavenly Father, we thank You.

For our home and our friends,
For playtime and work,
Dear Heavenly Father, we thank You.

For the flowers and trees,
For birds we hear sing,
Dear Heavenly Father, we thank You.

For the rain and the sun
That help things to grow,
Dear Heavenly Father, we thank You.

For Your Love that we know
Gives all things to us,
Dear Heavenly Father, we thank You.